THE

Room

THE
Room

Preparation for Prayer

ARCHIE MURRAY

PRAYING BELIEVERS SERIES

THE ROOM
Copyright © 2024 by Archie Murray

ISBN: 978-1-4866-2526-0
eBook ISBN: 978-1-4866-2527-7

Word Alive Press
119 De Baets Street Winnipeg, MB R2J 3R9
www.wordalivepress.ca

WORD ALIVE
—P R E S S—

Cataloguing in Publication information can be obtained from Library and Archives Canada.

Dedication

This first book on prayer is dedicated to all those believers throughout my life whose lives, particularly their prayers, inspired me from my youngest years. The memory of them still fills my heart with warm gratitude to God. Bill Steel praying at an all-night prayer meeting, or simply but movingly opening a Sunday morning service in prayer. The two Bobby Hamiltons. My own brother Robert, Peter Logie, Bobby and Jim Handyside, Matt Spears, Pastor Arthur Campbell, Raymond MacKeon. Many more whose names I have forgotten but who I still hear pouring out their hearts in prayer. Laying hold of the horns of the altar and crying out to God with tears. Their heart and mind engaged with God for revival in Scotland.

So many prayer warriors. So many ordinary hours turned into the "Gate of heaven." So many nights when we met simply to pray and only reluctantly stopped at a late hour, before continuing into the night in fellowship around the things of God. There were also many supportive women, young and old, with a similar burden for prayer. In those days, however, men by sheer numbers dominated the prayer meetings, unlike today.

Most of these wonderful people have gone to be with the Lord. A few remain and are still faithful till the end. May God replace them soon with a new generation determined to prove that God answers prayer. Because he most certainly does!

—Rev. Archie Murray

Contents

ACKNOWLEDGEMENTS

I want to express deep appreciation for my entire family who have unwaveringly supported me in writing and publishing my books. They have made the task a delight. Thank you to Word Alive Press, who have been so amazingly helpful with the publishing and editing and marketing of my books. Their understanding of my subject matter and message, and their attention to detail has been an essential part of this project.

Preface

I can only describe it as an "Ache." That is what caused me to write on prayer. Over many years, particularly since I entered the Christian ministry, this ache has become entangled with my experience of prayer both privately and in public church gatherings. Prayer was fundamental to my generation of believers. That is why in many churches the few remaining attendees are often elderly. The church says it believes in prayer, yet any critical examination would find us desperately falling short. Of course there are exceptions.

How to address the subject? I would love to travel the world preaching on the subject and making a call to prayer. While there are others more qualified who should be raising an alarm, I thought it would encourage the Lord's people if I were to write a brief and simple trilogy on prayer based on the Sermon on the Mount. This first book is about the much forgotten need to prepare ourselves to enter the presence of Almighty God. That is what this prologue to the Lord's Prayer deals with. That is why I have titled this book *The Room*. Jesus said, "Go into your room." The imagery presented by Jesus's choice of words is emancipating. Read it and believe it.

These are my own thoughts and limited for the sake of brevity to the basic understanding of prayer delivered to us by Jesus himself. There are three books in this series. The first is about preparation for prayer. The second book is based upon the pattern Jesus sets out in The Lord's Prayer. Then to inspire us further, the third book examines Paul's prayers in Ephesians to provide an aim for our intention to learn the practice of prayer. This we most certainly must regain.

INTRODUCTION

This little book is about an essential but often overlooked aspect of prayer: preparation. Have you ever felt when you finished praying that it was all over and done with before you realized it had even started? It can feel like taking medicine. Just gulp it down and don't think about it, either before or after. Just get on with your day! Do you ever feel like your prayer time is becoming pointless, but then wisely resist the thought? Preparation for prayer could change that.

Many people, due to desperate circumstances, are forced into praying. They are totally consumed by their own needs. They do not take time to consider who God really is, before or after they have prayed. Some wander in dreamingly just because they have set aside a certain time to pray. It can be as if heaven was just one part of the grand shopping mall of life. Others pray habitually and never examine the way they pray. They send requests to God, and that's all they understand prayer to be. But prayer is not just about asking for things desperate or regular, mundane or extraordinary. The Lord did not give us prayer to help us navigate a religious supermarket! He wants to fellowship with us. In that timeless time together, multiple levels of grace, mercy, and help are received. And our prayer is often answered before we even ask.

Others live a life that is constant preparation for prayer. Yet they still specifically prepare every time they pray. Every believer should prepare for prayer before saying a single word.

In this book I want to show that preparation is a real benefit to praying. The passage we will consider, taken from the Sermon on the Mount in Matthew chapter 6:5–9a, is like a prologue to Jesus's pattern for prayer which follows, beginning in chapter 6 verse 9b.

The people illustrated in this passage are timeless. The errors of the Pharisees are still with us today. The blessings of the poor sinner are still available for all who want to pray seriously. Do you?

Preparation for prayer is learning afresh who you are and who God is. Many believers have become so used to praying the way they do that they are offended by the suggestion that any critical thinking should be applied to prayer. Critical thinking here is only to be applied to our own prayers. Never be discouraged, never discourage another regarding their praying. Genuine prayers are heard by our heavenly Father. But growth is natural. What if there is no growth this year, or indeed over many years? Then maybe it is time to do some thinking. Set aside time for preparation as you go to pray today.

And when you pray, you shall not be like the hypocrites. For they love to pray standing in the synagogues and on the corners of the streets, that they may be seen by men. Assuredly, I say to you, they have their reward. But you, when you pray, go into your room, and when you have shut your door, pray to your Father who is in the secret place; and your Father who sees in secret will reward you openly. And when you pray, do not use vain repetitions as the heathen do. For they think that they will be heard for their many words. Therefore do not be like them. For your Father knows the things you have need of before you ask Him. In this manner, therefore, pray…

—Matthew 6:5–9a

Chapter 1
WHERE TRUE PRAYER BEGINS

Religion is about human beings seeking God… and not finding him. In the Sermon on the Mount, Jesus taught us how not to seek God and how to be found by him. He is already seeking us before we turn to him. We think we are trying to get the Lord's attention, but in reality he is the one trying to get our attention.

In Matthew 5 Jesus is speaking to a multitude of people about religion. He speaks about religion as it was on display in the lives of the Pharisees, a faction of religious leaders. Jesus identifies them in Matthew 6:5 as "hypocrites." He said their prayers would not be heard by God. The possible implications of Jesus's words here should be devastating for anyone who would describe himself as "religious." The idea that the prayers of religious people might not be heard is a radical sentiment.

Jesus told them plainly the root of this rejection. They were *hypocritical*. Hypocrisy is presenting yourself to be something you are not. The play actors in the Roman theatre wore costumes to create the illusion of a character. In doing so they hid their true selves. They often had large masks to further this deception. The masks had mechanical devises to increase the volume of the actor's voice, making them appear larger than they really were. It was all dissimulation. It must be noted that the audiences were willing participants, as theatre goers still are today. The Roman theatre might be excused seeing as the play was declared for what it was: an act.

In Matthew 6:5–9a we have a radical exposé of religion in terms of prayer. Not just a general observation, but a specific observation of the prayers of the Pharisees. This would be controversial enough if Jesus were speaking only to the laity. Yet, to further expose the extent of the hypocrisy, Jesus speaks of the Pharisees, the spiritual elite. These were those who had no excuse but who still persisted in this charade. What is the essence of the problem for Jesus? It is that their hypocrisy is delusional.

It is a delusion that has implications for the guilty party and for everything they touch. It demands that the listener becomes part of the act, which fails if they don't. If nobody takes it seriously (even at the level of mere play-acting) it fails to satisfy. Also, the more participants in the event, the more real it appears. The intention of the actor is to draw every observer into his part. He wants the audience to feel his emotions and to understand his love or his joy or his anger or his revenge. The listeners were to become party to the Pharisee's hypocrisy as he prayed.

This is all expected in a theatre where the environment is set up for entertainment. It is not intended to be taken seriously other than in its ability to please the audience. But prayer is not ever about an audience of mere human beings, no matter how engaged they are with another's prayers. The Pharisees, like

Shakespearian actors, were only acting out a part in a religious ritual. All that mattered was that people heard and saw their performance, and perhaps felt moved in some way. The whole thing was fake. The lifeless religious prayer of the Pharisee could not be examined. It was too fragile. It lacked the essential element of true prayer: reality.

Preparation for prayer begins with the discovery of the real you. To find the honest, balanced, and actual person you are. Indeed, what kind of *being* you are. Perhaps you are reading this book because you want to be a praying believer. The aim of this book is to discover what the essence of the praying believer is.

The essence of reality is found in God. Our view of ourselves is only real when examined in the presence of God. Outside of his light we deceive ourselves. We are like the man described in the book of James who looks at himself in a mirror, yet immediately forgets what he looks like (James 1:23–24). Yes, he sees something, but he goes away and chooses to listen to his excusing imagination. Human beings, even Christians, are often afraid to see themselves as God sees them. When God revives his church, he shows us the truth about ourselves. This truth only God can reveal. Scotland's national bard, the poet Robert Burns, summed this up well when he said, "Oh that God the Gift would give us to see ourselves as others see us" (my translation). He goes on to say that this knowledge would free us from "many a blunder," and from much that is ingenious among us, including "devotion."[1]

---

[1] Robert Burns, "To a Louse," in *Complete Poems and Songs of Robert Burns* (Glasgow: HarperCollins, 1995), 110–111.

David says in Psalm 139:23, *"Search me, O God, and know my heart."* Jesus said to the woman at the well in John 4:22–23, *"You worship what you do not know; we know what we worship… But the hour is coming, and now is, when the true worshipers will worship the Father in spirit and truth; for the Father is seeking such to worship Him."* God knows us. He sees us as we really are.

On the other hand, in Luke's Gospel Jesus says that an irreligious man, a "tax collector," who prayed, was heard. What was the difference that made one heard and another unheard?

Hypocrisy kills everything it touches. But part of the problem for the Pharisees is simply faulty preparation, or no preparation at all. The Pharisees spent no time preparing themselves, made no examination of themselves, and could not acknowledge the deadness of their religion, let alone the deadness of their conscience. They were secure in themselves. They felt no lack in themselves. The most dangerous place for believers to find themselves is trusting in themselves rather than God. The Pharisees had no preparatory thought about God, or they would have been terrified to ask in the way they did. What kind of blindness deceives a man into thinking he needs no preparation to meet God? It is a spiritual blindness coupled with the pride of religiosity.

Jesus said that the confidence of the Pharisees was faulty. Had they taken time to prepare before they went out into the marketplace, they would never have gone there. They would have discovered what kind of men they really were: sinners. They would also have discovered that God was not like them; he is holy. These thoughts would have dissolved their hypocrisy. Preparation opens our inner, spiritual eyes. The pharisees prayed comfortably blind to reality.

Yet, the Pharisees did sort of prepare, and they certainly prayed. But it was all a prepared performance for others to see. Their prayers never were about God! Their audience may have been moved; God was not moved. The Pharisees were not changed and their prayers were not answered. What a blasphemous waste of this precious gift of prayer!

The contrasting story of the tax collector is recorded in Luke 18:13–14, "*And the tax collector, standing afar off, would not so much as raise his eyes to heaven, but beat his breast, saying, 'God, be merciful to me a sinner!' I tell you, this man went down to his house justified rather than the other.*"

The sinner had prepared himself before he went to pray. He knew who God was and who he himself was. The distinction between himself and God humbled him, but God heard him. This preparation is the beginning of the Christian life, this awakened conscience. Prayer begins with this fear of God, coupled with a desperate desire to get right with him. The first prayer of the believer is shown to us here in the prayer of the tax collector: "God be merciful to me a sinner." The New Testament expands our understanding of this initial experience.

If your prayer life has dried up, start again here. Confession to God and repentance of heart are the prerequisites for a relationship with God. We must understand that forgiveness and cleansing are only available to us through the life, death, and resurrection of Jesus Christ. No good works or religious observance can bring us to God. Pray the "Sinner's Prayer." Read

Acts 16:31, "*Believe on the Lord Jesus Christ, and you will be saved.*" Read Romans 10:13, "*Whoever calls on the name of the Lord shall be saved.*" Receive Jesus as your saviour by faith and go and tell someone. Give your life to him. Pray every day. Read the Bible every day. Find a Bible believing church and get to know fellow believers. Leave this sinful world and live for Jesus every day. This is the beginning of true prayer. Being reconciled to God through Jesus Christ and walking in the light of his Word is the essence of the praying believer.

Preparation makes us think differently about ourselves and about God. It should make us real. As we look at this passage from the Sermon on the Mount, preparation is what we are thinking about. Even those who have been walking with God for decades need to prepare themselves for prayer by refreshing their relationship with God before they even reach their own private chamber to pray.

Preparation is where True Prayer begins.

When we are serious about something we prepare beforehand to maximize the benefit from it. Many people rush into God's presence and rush out again no different. The person who prepares before he prays will change the character of his praying. Preparation is not about improving yourself so that you are more acceptable. It is about preparing your heart, mind, and demeanor so that you are ready to meet God and to pray effective prayers. The Pharisee and the sinner both prayed. Only the sinner was heard. We too want to be heard.

Chapter 2
A Delightful Double Vision

Think before You pray. The following four points are general observations, helpful to preparation for prayer from the Sermon on the Mount.

When we intend to pray there is a *conflict* between faith and sight. Also, Jesus presents a *contrast* between the religious person and the believer, specifically in terms of prayer. This contrast reveals the praying believer to be a *distinct* kind of person. The praying believer, in his approach to prayer and in his praying, makes a *confession*. That is, a statement about what he believes. An awareness of these four things, *conflict*, *contrast*, *distinction* and *confession*, will help us to prepare for prayer.

Conflict

Prepare yourself. Faith and sight are always in conflict. This is especially true when we set out to pray. In The Sermon on the Mount, this conflict between faith and sight can be seen as an isolated individual speaking in plural terms. He is saying "our" Father, yet he is alone in an empty room. Faith sees God. Sight sees a sad, lonely individual! Faith has a delightful double vision. In preparation for prayer, faith in God, whom we cannot see, must overcome the misery we do see. Overcome in this moment of conflict, and many other potential conflicts will never arise.

The letter to the Hebrews says, "*But without faith it is impossible to please Him, for he who comes to God must believe that He is, and that He is a rewarder of those who diligently seek Him*" (Hebrews 11:6). Notice that our faith must be expressed as we "come" to God. That is, before we pray, in preparation. The exercise of solitary prayer is the source of the believer's public strength. Faith in operation in private prayer enables the believer to stand in the public conflict of ideas and temptations in the world. Faith is the victory that overcomes the world. "*And this is the victory that has overcome the world—our faith*" (1 John 5:4). The believer quickly learns that the mere inclination to pray ignites this conflict between faith and sight. So you must prepare beforehand. Set this attitude of faith in your heart and mind before you reach your secret chamber. Faith sees further than sight.

Private Faith
Produces Public
Strength

Chapter 3

CONTRAST: TRUE PRAYER IS NOT "RELIGIOUS"

Jesus reduces the Pharisee's public praying to a meaningless performance. His prayers are not heard. In contrast to the Pharisee, the poor sinner's prayer to God alone in the temple is heard, and he goes up to his house justified! Prepare for prayer like the sinner.

It is possible to pray with genuine faith in public and to receive answers. However, in terms of Jesus's teaching on prayer in the Sermon on the Mount, official public prayer would be the exception that proves the rule. The intention of prayer is not to bring God down into the presence of human beings, it is about lifting human beings up into the presence of God. Believers, as a norm, pray by faith and in secret. They are heard, answered, and rewarded openly.

Prayer is not about bringing God to us. Prayer is about bringing us to God.

Jesus contrasts the grand open spaces of the mountaintop in plain sight with a private room and a solitary individual. He contrasts the temple and the marketplace, the corners on busy streets with the secret chamber. In the secret chamber we shut out everyone but God.

The disciples had seen Jesus go away from them to pray. They had also heard him pray in their company. Something about his praying and his teaching on prayer made them want to pray like him. He did not pray like the religious leaders. There was a stark contrast. He talked to God they talked to other people. He was real, they were not.

When human beings reject the living God they invent dead religion. The difference is so evident that Jesus can easily reveal the contrast between believers and merely religious people. The secret place of prayer must be a place of stark, honest reality and pure simplicity. The place of prayer is not at all "religious." What a contrast this is!

In the secret place there is no need for performance. There is no oratory or drama, no posturing or articulation. There are no gestures, no practiced chant. No self-righteous hypocrisy. In this room it is impossible to hide. God is here.

Here there is no shade, no garments, no tinge or incense. There is nothing extraneous. There is nothing to further distort that which is already out of shape—*me!* Religion tries to hide us from God, but it fails to do so. It also tries to hide God from humanity. In this it often succeeds.

There is yet another contrast in prayer. Only two realities occupy this room: a sinful person and a holy God. It is a mercy that this is the case. In this private place a believer can embrace fully who he is. The believer is a poor wretched sinner, and he can be forgiven and cleansed. His confession of sin to God alone spreads no pollution.

When we have nothing but God, we have no need of anything but God.

Let us now also consider an encounter on another mountain between the prophet Elijah and the prophets of Baal. The prophets of Baal cry out, cut themselves, and make a lot of noise calling to their gods. Elijah says that perhaps their gods are sleeping and encourages them to shout louder (1 Kings 18:16–45). He knows that their gods are not real. He then does everything in precisely the opposite way, and fire falls on the altar when he prays. What a contrast! On this mountain there is no sense of panic or pain, even if our real circumstances seem to cry out for such. The place of prayer is filled with the peace and calm of real faith in the living God.

Real preparation produces real contrasts. It moves us from turmoil to equilibrium. Preparation brings a quiet, faithful trust in God. He will hear us because we have prepared to be alone with him. Returning to the Sermon on the Mount, we see that he will find us when we are nowhere to be found. He will find us in the solitary place before we have uttered even one word in prayer.

Notes

_____

_____

_____

_____

_____

Chapter 4
THE PRAYING BELIEVER: DISTINCTION

Paul and Silas are distinct because they are constantly prepared for prayer. This makes them a distinctly different kind of people. Learn to be like them and you will be prepared for prayer.

In the book of Acts we find Paul and Silas chained to the wall in a Roman prison. The Bible tells us they were praying! (Acts 16:16–40). It appears that whatever situation they found themselves in, they were comfortably ready to pray. Their natural response to everything was to bring it to the Lord in prayer. However, they were not asking for anything!

They were not pleading to be released or for their families to be comforted or for their wounds to be healed. This is a distinctly different kind of person. The individual who is prepared for prayer is prepared for anything but asks for nothing. When he has nothing, he prays as though he needs nothing, even when he is in chains and in jail! This prepared person will be heard. Paul and Silas were heard, and the Lord set them free in a spectacular way.

Paul and Silas were worshipping God, singing Psalms and spiritual songs. They were not asking for release or praying for revenge on their enemies. They were allowing the will of God to "be done on earth as it is in heaven." Did they want to be free? Only in the will of God. This is not remotely desperate. It is a beautiful, willing cooperation with "Our Father." Surely this sort of prayer shows that the believer is altogether different in kind from the religious person or the desperate person. He is a distinctly different person. He is a praying believer.

In John 4:23–24, Jesus says the Father is seeking those who worship in spirit and truth to worship him. Jesus is describing a believer who seriously wants to meet God. Indeed, who wants to know God personally, experientially. This impetus to pray comes from a relationship with God our Father.

The desire to commune with God and the amazing realization that God wants to commune with us is a change worked in us by God's Holy Spirit. This and many other character traits distinguish the believer from the unbeliever, making the one who prays a distinct individual. Recognize this about yourself before you pray. It is a work of God.

Notes

_____

_____

_____

_____

Chapter 5
BEHOLD HE PRAYS

The person who is set apart for prayer has been born again by the Spirit of God (John 3:3). He begins to seek after God with all of his being. He searches the Scriptures. Though he may have never prayed before, he prays now. This person is so changed that he has become a distinctly different being from before. He is daily preparing his heart to pray.

The secret place Jesus describes—the prayer room—calls him and he responds. Developing this responsive attitude is helpful preparation for prayer.

A beautiful example of this principle is found in the conversion of Saul of Tarsus, better known as the Apostle Paul. The story is told in Acts 9:10–19. Saul, a Jewish man, is on his way to arrest and even to kill the followers of Jesus of Nazareth. He thinks he is serving God! Then, on the Damascus Road he is knocked off his horse by a vision of Jesus Christ. Jesus speaks to him and shows him the error of his ways and reveals to Saul, that he, Jesus, is indeed the crucified, risen Christ, the saviour of sinners. Jesus tells Saul to go to a house in Damascus where a man will restore his sight, which he lost by the blinding vision. Saul goes there and waits.

Meanwhile, God speaks to a believer called Ananias and tells him to go and meet Saul. Ananias has heard of Saul and doubts this word from God! The Lord convinces him that a real change has occurred in Saul of Tarsus. The evidence God gives Ananias is simply, *"Behold he prays"* (Acts 9:11).

The forceful impression given to the reader is that this is a distinctly changed Saul of Tarsus; even his name will be different. Ananias prays for Saul and the story goes on to describe how Saul became the great Apostle Paul. Behold he prays! This praying distinguishes the believer from the unbeliever.

Notes

_____

_____

_____

_____

_____

Chapter 6
State What You Believe: Confession

Preparation for prayer is not confession of sin. It is a statement—a "confession"—of beliefs. The Nicene Creed (AD 325) and the Chalcedonian Creed (AD 451) are examples of the great historical statements of the Christian church's beliefs. We call them "confessions" because they openly and freely declare what we believe. Every believer is silently making his own small confessions when he goes into his room to pray. The pattern Jesus gave on the Mountain begins not with confession of sin but with an intentional confession that "God is."

What better preparation for prayer than to restate your belief in God, and your beliefs about him? Surely this stirs up faith and joy and strengthens the believer to pray. The act of praying begins with a confession declared by both our intention and the action of going to the place of prayer.

By withdrawing from the public eye to pray, this person silently declares his belief that "*God is*" (Hebrews 11:6). He makes this confession in the secret place before he ever makes it to the public. He believes God exists. And his intention to pray states his belief that God is relational.

His praying tells us God wants to talk with us, to work together, to walk together. This simple act of drawing near to God in prayer is a confessional statement. It also confesses that God is "*a rewarder of those who diligently seek Him.*" **(Hebrews 11:6)**

This expression of belief stirs up faith as we approach God. It is an act focused on God as God. It is a faith of submission and humility before God. True faith accepts the will of this God. It is a calm, comforting assurance. It is not dependent on any outcome. It is loving, willing submission to the will of God. This is preparation. The beliefs evidenced by our prayers may be very basic. They can also be very theological, even profound. Above all they must be generated by real faith. "*He that comes to God must believe that He is!*" (Hebrews 11:6). Jesus does get to confession of sin, but by the time we get there our confession is real. It is generated by a fresh vision of who God is and who we are in comparison with all his attributes and characteristics. Too often our prayers begin with a focus on our failure, and we remain in that mentality for the rest of our prayer time.

Such confession is natural and each of us makes a confession when we pray. The confession of the Pharisees was that their prayers were all about themselves. Often the words we use to make an impression are silently contradicted by our "confession." This confession is the message of our demeanour and our life, as seen by those who look on, certainly by God.

Chapter 7
SUPPOSITION OR PROPOSITION?

Our passage uses the phrase *"when you pray"* three times. Is this a supposition or a proposition? In the New Testament the Greek word for "when" is *otan*. This word can be used as a supposition, which comes with the expectation of failure, or it can be used as a proposition, which means that something will actually happen as proposed.[2] The language is clear, Jesus is not *supposing* that the believer *might* pray. He is *proposing* that the believer *will* pray.

This is very important for our understanding of believers and prayer. Jesus assumes that believers pray, and that prayer is so regular a practice for them that they can prepare for it well in advance. It is always on their mind. So, in effect believers are always preparing. They are thinking about the character and goodness of God. They are praising him, they are witnessing.

People who pray sporadically are not thinking about prayer. For them, prayer is not important enough to warrant preparation. Some only pray in response to stimuli like trouble or

---

[2] Spiros Zodhiates, *The Complete Word Study Dictionary, New Testament* (Iowa Falls: World Bible Publishers, 1992), 1067, 3752.

panic. Such people don't have time to prepare. They don't care about prayer as such. They only respond to that which is of immediate concern to them. Believers, on the other hand, pray like they breathe—naturally and regularly. Preparation is a constant possibility for the believer. The believer can always be preparing.

Prayer, like breathing, happens naturally. It has a pattern. It has structure and timing. It is necessary. It can be controlled, but it happens naturally. And when it ceases to be regular, it is in danger of ceasing altogether. Then something is seriously wrong! This natural expression of prayer is regular but not rigid. It allows for freedom of movement so that personal circumstances are able to be accommodated.

Notes

_____

_____

_____

_____

_____

Chapter 8
CUSTODIANS OF PRAYER

Let's consider again the phrase "When you pray." With that little word "you," we see that this is becoming personal.

During many seasons of the church's history, its members have been reduced to only a few praying people—often the elderly, and often women. These believers have been the custodians of true prayer when prayer hung in the balance, faced with possible extinction. But always a faithful few prayed. At such times the cold, ancient cathedral has been like a dead carcass, declaring itself to be the Christian church. However, it was just a stony shell going through the motions of religiosity without the life of God. God's people are seldom the majority. Jesus tells us that the "gate is narrow and the road is hard that leads to life, and there are few who find it" (Matthew 7:14).

Today in the Western world prayer is in danger of being silenced. What prayer remains has become heavy with too much need. Needs-based prayer is uncomfortably miserable, and many have given up on meeting with others for prayer because of this sense of misery. We need a renewed understanding of true prayer. These preparatory passages in the Sermon on the

Mount and the pattern Jesus gives in Matthew 6:6–9 give us a fresh approach to prayer.

These days preparing ourselves for prayer requires us to have survival instincts. Remind yourself as you begin to pray that everything may depend upon you praying in secret in your humble home. In difficult times the importance of the individual believer at prayer is further heightened.

Notes

_____

_____

_____

_____

_____

Chapter 9
PRAYING WITH INTENTION

The phrase "When you pray" foreshadows the teaching that is still to come in the Lord's pattern. It is sufficient to say that this word carries all the weight and the blessing of true prayer. It includes all the variations of experience and understanding. Those of you who have read and understood and learned from the Lord's pattern are who Jesus is describing when he says, "When you pray."

That little word "pray" demands engagement of one's heart, mind, and body. It is not the tension of fear or failure, but the application to a healthy task that can be accomplished. The text indicates action in prayer. It suggests individual work, effort, and accomplishment. We will never accomplish anything of worth without personal application to the task and the intention to succeed.

Imagine praying with the intention of real change. You intend to see a result and you refuse to give up until you know you have achieved something. Imagine the level of energy. Think about the interest level and the total engagement with the task of prayer. This must not be understood as creating some frenzy of human effort. Nevertheless, this is an aspect of the word "pray."

Prayer is fellowship with God and includes all the various aspects of real prayer that are in the Bible. There is something wrong if your prayers do not take any energy, or never activate deep desires and heart felt passion for God and humanity.

Too many prayers are never answered. Are answers the primary purpose of prayer? Not at all. Answered prayer is only one aspect of a certain type of prayer. But if our prayers don't convey to the Lord a serious intent, perhaps the Lord will withhold any answers we need until we learn how to pray!

Notes

_____

_____

_____

_____

_____

Chapter 10
TAMEION

"…go into your room…"

We are looking at the background and context of Jesus's teaching on prayer in the Sermon on the Mount. This is prior to Jesus delivering what we affectionately refer to as "The Lord's Prayer." We have seen that Jesus is addressing individuals among the group he is speaking to on the mountain.

At this point Jesus tells us about the place of prayer. He says, "Go into your *room*" (Matthew 6:6). Preparation for prayer includes finding, creating, and even defending a place for prayer. This clause has been understood in various ways. Some commentators suggest that it is merely a corrective to the public hypocrisy of the Pharisees who prayed in public spaces or in the temple to be seen by others.

Many religious people emphasize the *sense of place* above the actual meeting with God! Hence the decoration and furnishings of their "rooms." The praying believer above all wants to have fellowship with God. An imaginary sense of God inspired by images or furnishings will not do, nor are such things necessary to the life of faith. However, a place set aside for prayer is helpful. Hence, Jesus says "go into your room."

But I would add that it is not just the believer who longs for fellowship with his Father, but that the Father also wants fellowship with the believer, in private. This fellowship should be regular, uninterrupted by the affairs of others, and in this room.

Jesus advised believers to pray in a particular environment. However, we soon realize that the emphasis is not on the room itself, nor on its furnishings, decor or architecture. It is what the room affords the praying believer that is important—it is free from distraction.

A Sense of Place or The Presence of God?

Consider a congregation gathered in a great cathedral. They are often overcome with the *sense of place*, the overpowering ancient beauty of the decor, the statues, paintings, arches. But as they are engrossed in dead stone and the works of men, God himself may have come and gone without anyone ever noticing!

Jesus says, "*go into your room.*" It is enough for it to be a simple, unpretentious, bare room. In that room we can meet Almighty God and discuss the business of his kingdom in this world! We can also make a difference in this world by our time with God in prayer.

According to W. E. Vine, the Greek word *tameion,* which is here translated as "room," can mean "a private room," a room "where you will not be seen," or "any place of privacy."[3] Consider

---

[3] W. H. Vine, Merrill Unger, and William White, Jr., "Chamber" in *Vine's Complete Expository Dictionary* (Nashville: Thomas Nelson, 1985), 95.

these ideas for a moment. This is not just the careless use of a term to contrast with the public place. The word *tameion* implies privacy. Yet note that the room itself requires no unique spirituality or presence. It is according to Vine, "any place of privacy."

When this place is referred to as a "secret" place, it is not the place itself that is the secret. The believer's experience of God and his dealings with God are the "secrets" of the place of prayer. Boasting is not allowed.

The place itself must not be given any special character or importance. Any place that fits the general description will do. By implication, it can also be various places. It is not necessary to have just one place, although every place of secret prayer will have the same set of characteristics. There is nothing careless about the Lord's language here. It will generally be just an ordinary room in your home. But when used for prayer, it is transformed by faith into a special place, a *tameion*.

To find such a place is itself preparation for prayer. We may have to look for a long time before we can identify it. Yet all the while we are considering and measuring in our mind the meeting with God that this place will facilitate. This search is preparing for prayer. In this search we are diligently focused in our intention to pray. This does not, however, mean we cannot pray anywhere other than in such a room.

Jesus himself had to find a place to pray. He found it on mountains and in isolated crevices. Mountains and crevices still work. Hopefully, a quiet space in your home will be made available and will be respected by others while you pray. In every case, the searching for and finding of such a place is part of the preparation process. Note that no furnishings are called for. No atmosphere to be created. Nothing but God in heaven and the believer, God's ambassador, on planet Earth.

Notes

_____

_____

_____

_____

_____

Chapter 11
GOD'S WAREHOUSE

Interestingly and significantly, the word *tameion* also carries the meaning of "a warehouse or a storehouse."[4] What riches there are in the Lord's choice of words! Surely the place of prayer is a place where God's gifts are stored? Everything the believer needs to get to heaven can be found in the place of prayer! Dear reader, God has warehouses filled like Joseph's barns in Egypt. There is enough to fill your hungry soul. All your needs are there carefully stacked in order. Your name is already inscribed by God's own hand. It's all available in this simple room. Preparation for prayer means desiring this abundance. Understand, this abundance is all for God's children. Our approach to prayer must not be grasping or greedy but filled with faith.

God's blessings are spiritually substantial. There is more available here than you even realize you need. There are abundant blessings, waiting in motionless silence to meet the needs of praying saints in this storehouse, this *tameion*.

All the resources of the Godhead are on alert in this room. The divine machinery is permanently primed, waiting for a

---

[4] Vine, "Chamber," in *Complete Expository Dictionary*, 95.

prayer for daily bread. All goes into motion ushering answers to the tiniest, the frailest cry from the believer praying in this private place. There are seasons when the "staff" there are extremely busy. Other times there is not as much need. Sometimes the need is great but there are no calls for help. The best calls are for needs that can only be met by God himself. Surprisingly, there are luxury goods and necessities and everything in between. Because our Father knows who needs what, when, and how, you might not get what you want, but you will get what you need.

Find that place. Find it quickly. Prepare your heart and mind to identify it by considering the significance of your prayer time. As you search, let faith rise in anticipation of all the potential blessings and the help that is available there. Go there often and feed on the bread of life. Jesus is there. It is just a quiet little room. But when the door is closed and faith is engaged it is transformed. For that period of time it is made fit for a holy God to meet with a sinful human being.

Divine deals are done there. Decisions are ratified. Motives are examined. Hearts are changed as God deals with one of his children in the secret place. Forgiveness is there. Protection from evil is there. Even ordinary daily bread is there for those in need. The church today should take particular note that the humblest believer praying in the secret place can affect the course of nations, avert national disasters, turn nations to Christ, and evoke God's judgements upon the wicked. The presence of the room will stay with you till you return, sooner rather than later. This level of intentional preparation applied to prayer will transform a person before they even utter the words "Our Father."

No one leaves from here unchanged. Everyone is changed into the image of Christ. Every praying believer will lay down heavy burdens in this room, but will carry a different burden away with them. They will carry the burden of a genuine concern for God's glory, the fulfillment of his will, and the coming of his kingdom. After prayer, the lingering presence of the room will be bittersweet. Fellowship with God makes each one of us long for an end to the tyranny of evil in this world.

After prayer, to varying degrees, everyone halts, limping like Jacob on his thigh. Jacob's limp is an image of this abiding presence of God. Why a limp? Because we find ourselves even more out of step with this world having spent time with God in prayer. The worldly path is too rough, too uneven, too ungodly for the gait of the praying believer coming fresh from the presence of our Father in heaven.

All leave this secret room richer than they came. However, no one comes here looking for worldly riches. Those who seek the blessings of this world will never find them here. Instead, they find a different room of their own and decorate it. They make it up to look like something they know-not-what. Whatever it is in their mind, in reality it is a lie.

The greatest of this world's temples are cold and empty. The inspiring architecture only produces aspiring architects. Buildings cannot lead us to the throne of God. They are as cold as the great stones that built them. The religious experiences of the Pharisees only indicated that God had been there in a day gone by. When God's Spirit departs, a silent and condemning vacuum is left.

The believer's humble room needs no furnishings. It is furnished by the spirit of reconciliation and fellowship with God. It is too plain for the world's interests. They do not go there. Instead they are satisfied with the deadness of religious fantasy. They feel no need of a room, even if God is there.

Through the centuries many believers have benefitted from such rooms. The rooms themselves have been forgotten. Countless rooms where God met with his people. But they were never known, or they have since been forgotten. Those that have been identified have been turned into shrines for religious tourists and thereby desecrated. God was wise to keep these rooms secret. It's not the room that matters, it's who was in it. These are healthy thoughts in preparation for prayer.

Notes

_____

_____

_____

_____

_____

Chapter 12
THE DISCIPLINE OF ISOLATION

"…and when you have shut your door…"

Before you pray you must exercise the discipline of isolation. You must shut your door. We must create a place of peace. This is the quiet energy of faith in preparation. It is a settling of heart and mind preparing to meet God. We have come prepared, the moment of truth has now arrived, and it is time to close the door on all that is not necessary. All we need is a Bible and basic comforts. The less the better, but it's not important. Just shut the door. This is the decisive action by which you show the Lord that you are seriously interested in meeting with him.

The closing of the door is indicative of bringing a shutter down on everything else that concerns us, that interests us, or that clamours for our attention. Our troubles and our blessings must be left outside the door. What happens in this room when the door is closed is a secret dealing with God. In Matthew 6:6–9a Jesus tells us how to conduct ourselves while praying. But for now, we are still preparing for prayer so that we do not fall in and out of prayer unchanged.

Now that you are here, sit, stand, or kneel and wait a while. Soak up the silence. Even if there is no silence as such, *"bring every thought into captivity to the obedience of Christ"* (2 Corinthians 10:5).

Notes

_____

_____

_____

_____

_____

Chapter 13
SOAK UP THE SILENCE

Preparation is required to enter and to exit the room. When you close the door with intent, the devil sometimes predicts disaster in your world. He tells you that while you hide away to pray, your whole world will collapse in a heap without you. But "*he is a liar*" (John 8:44), ignore him. When you exit through the same door, you will find that things are different. Both blessings and troubles appear now to be more measurable, more balanced. Circumstances may not have actually changed. Rather, it is you that has been changed. Take note, the door of entry is also the door of exit. You may even hear trouble break out before you leave the room. Try to let it go, unless duty calls. Let it go and hold onto peace. Let that peace "*rule in your heart and mind*" (Colossians 3:15).

Notice that preparation is also required before exiting the room. We must reset before we leave this hallowed place. Here we are relaxed and blessed. Yet, the devil and the world have outposts right outside the door. Minions are employed to hinder us upon re-entry. They intend to destroy all the benefits we gained as we leave, to hurry us away to forgetfulness, and to weigh us down with a fresh set of burdens. The devil's minions try to draw us back into the problems we left outside the room before we entered. They don't mind what we do in the room, but they care a great deal about how we return into the battlefield of this world. They will attempt to rob you, distract you, and defeat you in your present state of blessing.

Unbelief is waiting to be your willing counsellor as you exit the door. We must be prepared for exit with the same diligence as we prepared for entry. Now that you have prayed, you do not have to pick up any of the burdens outside the room. You gave those burdens to the Lord. You may still have to engage with the practicalities, even be hurt by circumstances, but the burden and the heaviness is no longer there, because by faith you trust the outcome to be from the Lord for his own good purpose.

The Christian is diligent. Your prayer room can be the most tranquil place on earth. Yet now you are about to step out on to the battlefield again. Many believers want to stay longer in the room. Its atmosphere, its peace, its godliness warms them. As we leave the room, we are easy targets for temptation because, having experienced such peace, we are unprepared to reenter the fight. You must prepare for the after-prayer attacks upon your soul. Make sure you put on the armour of God. Be even more diligent than you were before you went to pray. "*Be sober, be diligent; because your adversary the devil walks about like a roaring lion, seeking whom he may devour*" (1 Peter 5:8).

Chapter 14
A Beautiful Conversation

"…pray to Your Father…"

At the beginning of the pattern Jesus offers, he tells us to be focused on God. He says firmly, "pray to your Father." Consider how much of our prayer is completely focused on ourselves and our own needs. Jesus shifts the focus of prayer from our own needs to God himself. Often our only preparation for prayer is to write down a list of our needs. Prayer that is focused on ourselves will have a short but expandable endpiece in the pattern. Preparation for prayer should not be preparing our own list of needs. True preparation is understanding God's list. Jesus shows this to us in his pattern for prayer. It begins with "Our Father."

The pattern is not one prayer among many. It is a different way of praying! It begins with talking to God about God. We acknowledge who he is: "our Father." We acknowledge where he is: "in heaven." In this way, prayer begins with worship. Entry to the presence of God without initial worship is superficial. In this pattern, Jesus highlights a few aspects of who God is in order to help us. He is introducing the disciples to an entirely different approach to God. In this one word, "Father," we see that God is both almighty and comfortable.

Right at the beginning we are told that prayer is to be addressed to "our Father." What a beautiful conversation we can expect to have with him. In this simple address, we also learn something about being fathers, as well as about being children. God is the original Father. What do you expect when you go to prayer? Before you blurt out your own agenda, prepare, prepare, prepare.

Notes

_____

_____

_____

_____

_____

Chapter 15
GOD'S REWARDS

"… and your Father who sees in secret
will reward you openly…"

God in secret, rewarding us openly, what are we to expect? God's rewards often come in the form of our own character development. He rewards us with spiritual formation and growth in sanctification. True, God's rewards can be monetary or physical gifts. Yet the believer should not look for—or expect—temporal blessings. When Jesus says that God rewards us openly, he means in a way that will be made manifest to all.

The word *reward* is difficult in the modern world because we think too much in monetary terms. The intention is to encourage us to know and look for a good response, a beneficial answer, to our prayers made in secret. More to the point, we should seek an answer that is clearly identifiable as coming from the Lord. Jesus also wants us to clearly know that prayer brings about good for those who pray and those we pray for.

While we may not even realize when we have been rewarded, others will see us being changed into his image. We should not confuse "openly" with the goods of this world. The reward can be material blessings, but spiritual rewards are always best. Even the worldly person admires these things in the believer's life. The worldly person is envious of the believers strength, even without knowing that this strength is a gift from God. We should never forget that these gifts are freely given from God. We acquire them just by being in his presence in prayer. They are not the result of our accomplishments; they are expressions of his free grace.

Be prepared for prayer to produce change in your heart and mind, and in your daily life. Watch for it. His rewards are often not what we expect. Use them to advance his kingdom. Perhaps he will reward you with a generous spirit. If you are not prepared to receive his generous rewards, you might just remain Scrooge-like.

Notes

_____

_____

_____

_____

_____

Chapter 16
LISTEN TO YOURSELF

*"And when you pray, do not use vain
repetitions as the heathen do."*

Jesus's teaching is, in part, a response to the errors of the religious community, especially the religious leaders. Yet if we are honest with ourselves, we know that we have a similar tendency to use many superfluous words when we pray. Preparation for prayer includes awakening an attitude of thoughtful, intelligent expression.

This suggestion is so close to the idea of pre-written prayers that I must object to my own words! I must emphasize that only prayer that is from the heart pleases God. He would rather you blurted out incoherent, rambling thoughts from your heart than that you read a beautiful, prepared speech. This is especially true if someone else wrote it. Rather, learn to say what you mean and mean what you say. Listen carefully to yourself as you pray. Remember, you are talking to your heavenly Father.

More cuttingly, Jesus said, "do not use vain repetition." Some commentaries suggest that this means *heathen* babbling. But the Pharisees were not babbling heathens. They were learned religious men, devout and thoughtful in their religion and seriously pernickety about its practice. Yet Jesus describes their prayers as vain repetition. They did not humble themselves in consideration of who God is—the God to whom they believed they were praying. They did not search their hearts as they went out to the marketplace. Instead they checked their robes, adjusted their facial expression, put on their religious demeanour, and prepared their vocal cords. Yet, their heart remained as hard and cold as the temple blocks. Religious performance requires no faith, only repetition.

Jesus's teaching on prayer implies that we should give preparatory thought to every aspect of our prayer, yet not to kill our spirit. Instead, consider what you will bring before God and give thought as to how to express what is on your heart. You do not have to learn theological jargon. However, some serious reading will facilitate praying with clarity.

In the final analysis, listen to yourselves as you pray in order to develop better expression and clarity. Perhaps you might start afresh, thoughtfully addressing the Almighty. Our public prayer reflects our private prayer. If we require notes in order to pray in public, perhaps this reveals a lack of thoughtful prayer in private. There are many good examples of prayer recorded in Scripture, both in the Old and New Testaments. We can learn from all of these examples. But Jesus's teaching surely comes first.

Allow me a caveat to my insistence on extempore prayer. One exception to this rule would be if you are involved in a public meeting in an official capacity. This might be a wedding or a funeral or a government occasion. In these instances there is a need for accurate speech. It is legitimate to prepare your own written prayer in advance or to use a well-prepared prayer from a good source. This is especially the case when under serious pressure or when reputations might be tarnished by being unclear or inarticulate.

Notes

_____

_____

_____

_____

_____

Chapter 17
COME AND REASON

*"For they think that they will be heard
for their many words."*

We are perhaps not surprised at what Jesus said about the Pharisees. However, his words are for us to consider as well. This phrase can mean different things when applied to different people. In the case of the Pharisees they thought they would be heard for their many words. For others "many words" can be an indication of doubt and fear that God will not listen. Prayer can be a last, desperate attempt to find help—there are no atheists in a storm. God answers according to his own purposes. Because he is a merciful God, he even hears the cry of the genuine unbeliever. Every day he *"sends rain on the just and the unjust"* (Matthew 5:45).

Here a word of caution is called for regarding prayer meetings in Bible believing churches among real believers. The use of many words in prayer can suggest that one is desperate to be heard. He is our Father. He wants to hear our prayers and he loves to lavish us with his care. Any repetition that suggests that God is reluctant to respond is to be avoided. Passionate appeals are to be expected during difficult circumstances, so long as our passion is about our need and not from fear that God will not hear us.

God invites us to come and reason with him about our relationship with him: *"'Come now, and let us reason together,' Says the Lord, 'Though your sins are like scarlet, They shall be as white as snow; Though they are red like crimson, They shall be as wool'"* (Isaiah 1:18).

If you have never had this pointed conversation with God about your relationship with him, then it is imperative that you do so at once! Why is it urgent? In terms of preparation for prayer, because God will not hear you until your relationship with him is restored.

Our relationship with God has been broken by our sins. There is in fact nothing we can do within ourselves that will change this. He says, *"Come let us reason together."* He wants to tell you about his son Jesus Christ, who paid the price for our sins and made salvation a free gift. Jesus bore the wrath of God for you. We must repent of our sins and put our trust in him so that we may be forgiven and cleansed and made acceptable to God. That's what being reconciled to God is all about. This reasoning is the preparation for our first real prayer. It will be heard, like the prayer of the sinner in Jesus's story, and it will receive an answer. Even the shortest prayer of repentance, offered in response to God's offer of free salvation, will be answered. This answered prayer will be evident in the life and experience of the sinner who prayed.

Chapter 18
STRENGTH IN AN INDEPENDENT MIND

"Therefore do not be like them."

Prepare for prayer by developing the strength of an independent mind. Do not pray to be seen or heard by any other person. Do not mimic the prayers of anyone else. Have no care about what others think of your praying. Pray to your Father. Do not try to impress him with your knowledge or your words. Never allow yourself to get into an act. We are all capable of deluding ourselves. Learn to be honest; learn to be brief. God is not afraid to hear your honesty. Read the Psalms and there you will discover what honest prayer is like.

The Pharisees had no faith. They thought prayer was about the words they used. Prayer is about God. The Letter to the Hebrews says, "*He that comes to God must believe that He is, and that He is a rewarder of those who diligently seek Him*" (Hebrews 11:6). When you pray, believe that you are in the presence of God, and that he is listening.

Almost anything human beings do repeatedly can become mind numbing. It takes great effort to keep things fresh despite repetition. Generally, repetition produces mindless people. This is true of every situation in life that becomes repetitive. Prayer is no different. Even if you have been praying as a believer for decades you will find that there are things you say to God without thinking. They have become habit. Don't say anything if you aren't able to say it with your heart and mind in tandem. Remember, you are talking to God.

Notes

_____

_____

_____

_____

_____

Chapter 19
GOD KNOWS EVERYTHING

*"For your Father knows the things you have need of,
before you ask Him."*

As you prepare for prayer, consider that God knows your needs before you even ask. Do not pray as if God was ignorant of the facts of your life. Talk to God who knows everything intimately, even your sins. Still, he wants to fellowship with you, one to one. This is amazing! He is your Father, who is in heaven.

God knows what we need before we ask. This does not make our requests redundant. However, it raises the question as to their purpose. John Calvin's commentary on this verse is helpful. He writes,

> But if God knows what things we have need
> of before we ask Him, where lies the advantage
> of prayer? Believers do not pray with the view
> of informing God about things unknown to
> Him, or of exciting Him to His duty, or urging

> Him as though He were reluctant. On the con-
> trary they pray, in order that they might arouse
> themselves to seek Him, that they may exercise
> their faith in meditating on His promises, that
> they may relieve themselves of their anxieties by
> pouring them into His bosom… that they may
> declare that from Him alone they hope and ex-
> pect, both for themselves and others, all good
> things.[5]

We must avoid hijacking God's agenda and injecting our own. Those things which concern us are not irrelevant, but Jesus gave us a better way of addressing them by his pattern. Preparation for prayer reminds us of these great principles. As we pray, the reasons for prayer should be fresh in our mind so that we do not get lost in our emotional needs.

The disciples had seen and heard both the Pharisees and Jesus praying. Jesus's prayer was attractive because it was different! The disciples did not want to pray like the Pharisees. They wanted to pray like him. Do you?

Often we bring into our prayer time the unexamined assumption that God is ignorant of our needs. It is as if he needed us to supply all the details of what is going on in our life. We feel the need to bring him up to date with every detail of events. Then we move on to pleading, which suggests that God is reluctant to help us. Eventually, we praise him and thank him, but

---

[5] John Calvin, *Calvin's Commentaries, vol. 16: Harmony of Matthew, Mark, and Luke* (Grand Rapids: Baker, 1974), 314.

only because we believe it will encourage him to help us. And as we conclude our prayer time, our expectation is that God will do what we told him to do. And we believe that will be the best outcome. We expect that God will help us and answer our prayers in the way that we ask him to.

None of these intentions are pre-meditated. They are a result of our lack of clear preparatory thinking, furthered by a misunderstanding of God, ourselves, Christianity and the world. Jesus knows this and has provided the pattern to guide us.

Reformed theology emphasizes, rightly, that God is above all things. All the ancient men and women of God held his name, reputation, and interests in high esteem. The glory of God is an essential matter, to be preserved at all costs. Consider Joshua's prayer after the defeat of Ai. He prays, "*The Canaanites and the other people of the country will hear about this and they will surround us and wipe out our name from the earth. What then will you do for your own great name?*" (Joshua 7:9). Joshua is concerned about Israel's name being wiped out because it will lead to God's great name being defiled.

This emphasis on the name and glory of God must be restored in the church. Jesus's pattern will guide us to this and others similar principles which we may have forgotten, and which will restore power to our prayer. In preparation for prayer, we must meditate on the examples given to us in Scripture, and so culture ourselves according to the same pattern.

Notes

_____

_____

_____

_____

_____

Chapter 20
PATTERN OR PRAYER?

This is a suitable place to raise the question, Is the Lord's Prayer found in Matthew 6:9–13 a *set prayer*, or is it a *pattern* to guide us when we pray? This distinction will help us maintain a proper approach to prayer as well as to the pattern.

Many believe that this is a prayer intended for public recitation. However, simply put, the public place is categorically rejected by Jesus! Jesus says, "Go into your chamber... shut the door, [and] pray to your Father who is in the secret place." (Matthew 6:6). This is a guide, a pattern for the individual to use in private prayer. Does this mean it is wrong to have, for example, a school assembly recite the Lord's Prayer? Not necessarily.

In the preface to his work, *The Lord's Prayer*, the Puritan Thomas Watson, makes a clear and helpful statement that is worth quoting. Commenting on the phrase, "After this manner," he says, "Jesus gave to His disciples and to us a directory for prayer... The Lord's Prayer is the pattern of our prayer... Christ here has prescribed a pattern of prayer... the meaning is, let this be the rule and model according to which you frame your prayers." He continues, "we ought to examine our prayers by this rule." Finally, he says, "Let your petitions agree and symbolize with the things contained in the Lord's Prayer."[6]

We are at liberty to recite any passage of God's holy Word in public. This has been done in the past to teach the pattern to those who could not read or who had no Bible. Jesus is teaching us that the art of prayer can only be learned by the act of praying

Notes

_____

_____

_____

_____

_____

---

[6] Thomas Watson, *The Lord's Prayer* (London: The Banner of Truth Trust, 1965), 1.

Chapter 21
It Is the Most Used Prayer

This pattern has often been used as a set prayer. That is, it has been recited without embellishment for generations. It was embedded in cultures across the world for centuries.

It has been revered by the greatest of kings and the poorest of the poor. It has been recited at grand royal assembles and ordinary family meals. Today, the Lord's Prayer is recited in school rooms, at hospital beds and in millions of churches around the world. Atheists and ancients, soldiers and caregivers, all bow their heads when they hear the Lord's Prayer. It needs no introduction. It is beloved by countless societies, and many societies have been shaped by its principles. It is still loved and revered by those that use it.

It is the most used of all the prayers in the Bible. Yet, in the Bible there is no recorded instance of it being used as a set prayer. Other prayers contain seemingly richer language. Some are more theological, others are more emotional. There are many that are more dramatic, even desperate. Some are filled with faith. Others are more worshipful, more exalting than the Lord's Prayer. Some are filled with love, others express a simple need for daily help. Yet this prayer outstrips them all in daily use, both in the history of the church and in society. In public and private prayer, this prayer rises above all others. Even where liturgies and set prayers are rejected, this prayer is often recited. When prayed genuinely, its richness is undeniable. But Jesus intended something more for this prayer than mere poetic wonder. He intended a pattern of genuine prayer fulfilling its proper function and facilitating fellowship with God.

However, it is generally true that repetition works against fellowship with God. The spoken word of God can quickly be reduced to mere poetry. Worse yet, it can become a mindless, hypnotic mantra.

When the pattern becomes the prayer, it becomes lifeless and so do we. The pattern itself is like the paper pattern of a beautiful dress or a drawing of a flower. Both are lifeless. The flower on the page has no sweet room-filling aroma. It has no depth, no movement. The dress is empty and is literally lifeless!

Reality contributes to the space it occupies. The real flower with a beautiful fragrance, the real dress with a beautiful bride. Reality has it all. It gives more than it takes. It fills more space than it occupies. It has presence that demands attention. It has life itself.

The believer should use this pattern to shape and inspire his own words when he is praying. It is only then spiritually uplifting. When understood correctly, this pattern will carry us from the empty room into heaven itself. It will take us into heaven and bring us all the way back to earth a changed person. It will help us to engage with God himself.

Prayer following this pattern is pleasing to God and beneficial to men. It is this practice that has made prayer so special in the life of the Church. Many believers today have no idea what prayer is supposed to achieve. Many imagine they do know, yet they never achieve anything!

Notes

_____

_____

_____

_____

_____

Notes

_____

_____

_____

_____

_____

Chapter 22
IT IS THE MOST ABUSED PRAYER

The Lord's Prayer is also the most abused prayer in the Bible. It is abused because misuse of that which we revere is abuse. In the case of the Lord's Prayer, this misuse is close to blasphemy. Blasphemy is the careless use of God's name.

The Lord's Prayer is often recited without heart or mind. It is spoken without belief or faith. Such misuse far exceeds the occasional genuine soul who, in humble desperation, reverently invokes the words of the Master. The Lord hears our heart above our words. The occasional misuse may be understandable. The institutional enforcement of misuse by those who should know better is inexcusable. What exactly is this misuse?

The misuse is presenting a pattern as the final product. It is like a tailor selling the paper pattern as the finished garment, ready and fit for use as it is! It is the claim that the teaching of Jesus in Matthew 6 is the final word on prayer, in the form of a "ready-made" prayer. The Lord's teaching on prayer was not—is not—merely a set of words to be spoken in prayer. Prayer is more substantial than that.

Those who view the pattern as a prayer should recognize that it is lacking in many aspects. Almost all of its component parts beg for more to be said. This alone reveals it to be a pattern to be examined and understood. Once understood, we can then introduce its principles into our own private prayer.

As a set prayer, it does not allow for my heart's expression. In essence, we are excluded by having to use someone else's expression and words. What sort of conversation am I having with God if I only speak to him with a prepared set of words? The understanding that the Lord's Prayer is to be a set prayer is simply untenable. The context of Jesus's teaching further denies the idea of it being a set prayer. The entire context is about a private individual in a private, even secret, room talking to God in person. Who reads a prepared set piece in a private conversation?

Public recitation of this pattern as though it represented a real expression of prayer is a misuse of a beautiful pattern given to us by Jesus. Such near-universal recitation makes it the most abused prayer in the Bible.

Notes

_____

_____

_____

_____

_____

Chapter 23
IT IS THE MOST IGNORED PRAYER

The most used, the most abused, and also the most ignored. How so? Simply because countless believers have not sufficiently considered the actual teaching of this pattern. We have not been interested enough in the art of praying to learn from this pattern. God wants to listen to *us* praying. And when we ourselves genuinely pray, he does listen. Never doubt that. Even though we are often not beautiful or deep or poetic in our praying, he does listen. We are seldom profound. Few of our interests in prayer will shake the world. Sometimes, despite their lack of substance, our prayers are not even concise. Still, God wants to hear us as we are. He gave us this pattern to enable us to learn to pray acceptably and more effectively.

The true beauty of prayer is not clever language. The true beauty of prayer is from the heart. While the two are not mutually exclusive, they often conflict. Jesus's pattern fulfills the need of all real believers to learn to pray. Our prayers will still be humble, and we will be using our own words. But our prayers will engage our whole being with God, and we will receive answers for our own needs and much more. They will usher in the kingdom of God.

Today, were we to ask Jesus to teach us to pray, he would direct us to Matthew 6. Jesus gave this pattern to the disciples to meet their sense of need and to guide them in their praying. The disciples did pray, yet they were not happy with their prayers. For this reason they asked for help. Perhaps they wanted their own prayers to resemble Jesus's prayers. They had heard and seen him pray many times.

We too can learn from the pattern. Have you ever looked at it and compared your own prayers? I have asked many believers this question and no one has answered yes. Most have been bewildered by the question. We have simply ignored the Lord's pattern. It is his guide on "how to" (Greek: *houtō*) pray.

Notes

_____

_____

_____

_____

_____

Chapter 24
THE "HOW-TO" OF PRAYER

"In this manner…"

"The greek word *houtō* used here may be translated, "in this way" or "after this manner." Here Jesus is simply using it in order to teach us "how to" pray.[7]

Our approach to prayer matters. How should we enter the presence of God? Jesus says, "In this manner…" Often, we fall clumsily into the presence of God. There is a growing number of needs demanding our attention and weighing heavily upon us. Like a beggar's baggage they trip us up as we enter the holy of holies. The place of prayer is a glorious place. Yet too often we enter without navigation and recount an incoherent list of needs. The pattern eradicates our needs. It liberates us from them. By design, this pattern Jesus gives to us empties us of needs and fills us with God himself. Before we ask for anything, we find we have received him!

Preparation for prayer is what this book has been about. It is about raising the experience of prayer to a higher level in the

---

[7] Vine, "manner," in *Complete Expository Dictionary,* 391.

life of the individual and the church. Often our prayers have shrunk to the miserable repetition of one word, "help." Follow the pattern and our prayers will be a glorious expansion of another word, "Father!"

May the Lord bless this little book to your soul.

Notes

_____

_____

_____

_____

_____

You may contact me with any comments or questions you may have. I would love to hear from you. My email address is archiemurray7@gmail.com.

Notes

_____

_____

_____

_____

_____

Author Bio

Since his conversion to Christ in his early teens, Archie Murray has been fully engaged in the life of the evangelical Churches. Since his conversion he has been a follower of Jesus Christ. This conversion came with all the freshness (and ignorance) found in those who become Christians from a non-Christian background. The freshness has never left. The ignorance, he corrected by serious study of the Bible and Christian literature from his early teens, and by regular hearing God's Word proclaimed by godly men.

In later life, in order to better understand the Scriptures, he studied full-time for nine years, seven of which were in the divinity faculty of Glasgow University, including three years at the post-graduate level. There everything he believed was challenged and at the same time ratified, with the support of the history of the Christian church and the writings of the great men of the past. His understanding of Christianity was ratified, not destroyed, by the critical approach to the Bible. However, overall, he found it to be lacking. He found his own experience of God reflected in the lives of saints throughout time, and his own faith was proved through opposition. It must be acknowledged that—but for a few—the faculty were supportive of his Christian experience and understanding.

Prayer has been a constant and essential element of his Christian life. In his youth, prayer fuelled godly enthusiasm and controlled excess. Prayer formed his attitude and informed his responses to various experiences, good and bad. On every occasion, prayer was the essential element in correcting and reviving his soul. In prayer he has met God again and again. It is the reality of communion with God that has restored and revived passion for Christ and his cause. While all the other means of grace have contributed to his life experience, prayer is the one constant that has brought this beggar close to the Lord and lifted him from the mud of life and set him on his feet rejoicing. For these reasons he chose to write on the much used, much abused, and much ignored words of The Lord's Prayer. Perhaps his experience and teaching can bring you to similar heights from your depths. There can be no refreshment for your soul without true prayer.

Notes

_____

_____

_____

_____

_____

OTHER BOOKS BY ARCHIE MURRAY

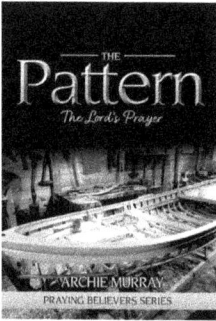

The Pattern (978-1-4866-2215-3)
What is so special about this pattern for Prayer? It is the most comprehensive succinct simple yet profound detail on prayer. It liberates. It lifts both prayer and prayer to the highest level. It takes the mundane and lifts it to glorious richness. It lifts us out of ourselves, an essential need for every generation but none more than today. It is divine guidance for praying. Both in the practice and in content and focus of true prayer. It contrasts violently with much of our praying. It raises us to a high level. It demands faith in action in prayer. It rewards with answers never experienced by the mundane formal repetitive dryness of the religious observance of rules. It does not contain rules. It is life giving. It both reaches heaven and takes us there too. More pertinently, it lifts those we pray for right into the presence of God. Would you experience real prayer? If yes…follow the pattern with all your heart soul mind and strength. Not as something to superimpose on your praying. But, as a guide shows you the way up the mountain, you more confidently set your step to reach the goal. The goal of Praying is not to get things. It is to meet with Almighty God, Our Father, to stay there until our conversation and appeals have been heard. Until we are changed. I offer this little treatise with a humble confidence that it can assist any who take it seriously to grow and grow and grow throughout the rest of your days in the grand privilege of Prayer.

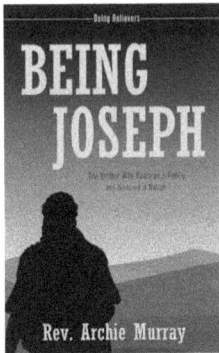

Being Joseph (978-1-4866-1573-5)
Have you ever felt betrayed by a family member? Have you ever needed even a glimpse of hope to help you through a tough situation? In the Old Testament, we read that Joseph was thrown into a pit and then sold by his own brothers. This great betrayal left him feeling alone and in despair. Unfortunately, this was only the beginning of his troubles.

Being Joseph takes a closer, pastoral perspective on perseverance through hardships, the value of forgiveness even when it's near impossible, and the redemptive hope of reconciliation. Joseph's story expands on dreams, slavery, seduction, imprisonment, and the restoration of a family. In the worst moments of Joseph's life, we can see that God never left his side. The lessons we can learn from this book can help enrich our daily lives in this difficult world today.

All ages will benefit from this captivating commentary on a real family, just like yours.

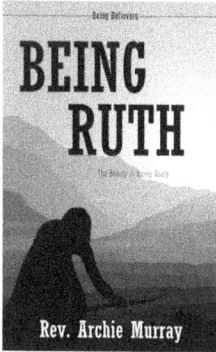

Being Ruth (978-1-4866-1709-8)

Have you ever felt like your faith was being tested? Have you ever experienced the death of a loved one? The book of Ruth, found in the Old Testament, is a moving story of a sad tragedy followed by an unrelenting commitment, both human and divine. Ruth's sadness is followed by hope deferred, yet undeterred.

Being Ruth takes a closer pastoral perspective on the shape of human expressions and relationships, the significance of names, and the consequences of men dying childless. We see Ruth, the committed daughter-in-law to Naomi, responding with grace during a difficult time in life. Although this is not your typical love story, as you allow the Scriptures to speak you'll find a beautifully enchanting story.

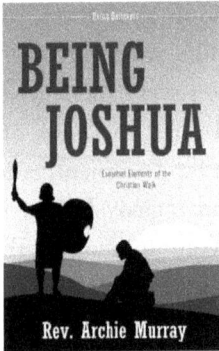

Being Joshua (978-1-4866-2213-9)

Have you ever wanted to be stronger, more vibrant, as a believer? Have you ever felt the church is weak when it should be strong? Have you ever felt that rampant evil should be shut down? Do you believe change is possible in the world, in the church… in you?! Joshua experienced a bad start in life—forty years in slavery. He wandered a desert for another forty years. Yet it was in and from these experiences that he discovered the believer's strength. He escaped slavery and went on to shut evil down and conquer the Promised Land. If we want to conquer the world for God… we must allow God first to conquer us.

Being Joshua shows how God uses the circumstances of life to change us into who He wants us to be. In life's slavery and wanderings, Joshua teaches us how to synapse with God's Spirit. Joshua teaches us that God is doing something—we are a part of it, but it is bigger than us. Joshua teaches us how to view life within the purposes of God and gain victory over our circumstances and ultimately ourselves. Joshua shows us that the weakest and the strongest believers need to encourage themselves and be strong. He reminds us, pertinent to our times, that we must also encourage each other. Joshua learned this from the Old Testament Scriptures taught in a godly family life, a community of believers, and a personal walk of faith in God. His education was by words and examples in real daily life. This book is written from a pastoral and practical perspective.

Watch for the next book in the
Praying Believers Series: The Practice!

www.ingramcontent.com/pod-product-compliance
Lightning Source LLC
Chambersburg PA
CBHW071622040426
42452CB00009B/1450